Bushy Park

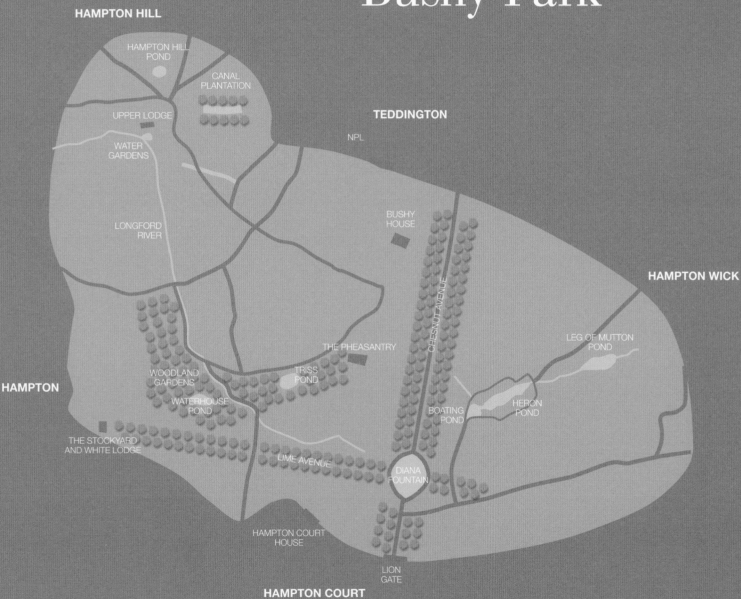

HAMPTON HILL

HAMPTON HILL POND

CANAL PLANTATION

UPPER LODGE

WATER GARDENS

TEDDINGTON

NPL

LONGFORD RIVER

BUSHY HOUSE

HAMPTON WICK

HAMPTON

THE PHEASANTRY

CHESNUT AVENUE

LEG OF MUTTON POND

WOODLAND GARDENS

TRISS POND

WATERHOUSE POND

BOATING POND

HERON POND

THE STOCKYARD AND WHITE LODGE

LIME AVENUE

DIANA FOUNTAIN

HAMPTON COURT HOUSE

LION GATE

HAMPTON COURT

a year in the life of bushy park joanna jackson

a year in the life of **bushy park** joanna jackson

unity
Print & Publishing

To Ben and Jake with love.

Thanks to:

Annie Murray and the 'Friends of Bushy Park'

All the park staff at White Lodge

My friends for their help with choosing the front cover

Miche for proof-reading

Pictured right: Bluebells, the King's River Garden,
Woodland Gardens

contents

introduction

Described as the 'Palace playground', Bushy Park's history has for the last 500 years been inexorably linked to Hampton Court Palace. At 1,100 acres it is the second largest of London's Royal Parks, the little sister to the nearby Richmond Park. Locals are blessed with a plethora of beautiful parks on their doorsteps. While Richmond Park is hilly and undulating, Bushy is flatter and was over many hundreds of years used for agricultural purposes. It was settled over 4,000 years ago with archaeological finds dating back to the bronze age. In its north west corner there remains the remnants of medieval feudal field systems.

The area remained common land spread over several parks until Henry VIII took over Hampton Court Palace from Cardinal Wolsey in the early 16th century. Henry appropriated the land, enclosed it and made himself a wonderful deer park where he could indulge in one of his favourite pastimes – hunting. His first act was to chop down many mature oak trees to build ships for his navy, but with foresight he also planted many new saplings and surrounded them with prickly hawthorn bushes to protect them from being nibbled by the deer. It is believed that these bushes gave the park its name.

Later kings and queens shaped the parks architecture and flora and fauna. Charles I had the Longford river built to supply his palace with extra water. William III landscaped the park, adding chestnut and lime avenues and the Diana fountain. The future William IV cut 758 trees down to make some extra cash, stripping the park of nearly all its trees in the process. He redeemed himself later when he became a bit more flush with money and re-planted some oak copses and then to celebrate his coronation opened the park and the Palace to the public. It has remained a popular public place to visit ever since.

Due to a generous donation by the Heritage Lottery Fund, over the last few years the Water Gardens, the Diana Fountain and the woodland gardens have all been restored to their former glory. The Pheasantry cafe has been made into a lovely space to enjoy some welcome food and drink after a wander through the park, enjoying all it has to offer. However, the increased visitor numbers bring with them their own problems.

The future holds major challenges for the park superintendent and his staff. A fine balance to keep the park as natural as possible at the same time as making it a wonderful place to visit is a constant tightrope they have to walk. The acid grasslands are protected because of their rarity but are under threat from dog faeces, which, if left on the ground and not picked up contaminates the soil. Acid grasslands need a deprived, nutritionally poor soil to thrive.

What's more, the deer need room to roam and behave as semi wild animals without being crowded by fascinated onlookers. However, probably the biggest challenge is the threat to the ancient woodland: the perfect home for the nationally rare stag and click beetles, are the avenues of lime and chestnut trees. If acute oak decline, ash dieback and bleeding canker, which affects horse chestnut and lime trees, take hold and kill off many trees, the park will change beyond belief. Hopefully all these conundrums will be dealt with and Bushy Park will flourish in the next 500 years, as it has in the past.

Early morning Autumn mist at the appropriately named 'Heron Pond'

winter

Top right: little grebe

Harsh conditions for the wildfowl on the watercourses of the park.

The Longford River

In fact, The Longford River isn't a river at all, but a canal. Strangely, although Hampton Court Palace is situated next to the River Thames, in the past its household was always short of water. Drinking water was pumped from a conduit at Coombe Hill and several local springs supplied the palace fountains. However, these springs often dried up in hot summers and the ponds in the gardens had to be kept full by labourers working at night. They worked manually using a treadmill, hauling water up from wells to re-fill the water features.

It was decided by the powers that be that it would be a good idea to construct an artificial waterway from the Colne river to provide an extra and reliable supply of water to the garden. This engineering feat was overseen by the contractor, Edward Manning, who had already done work in nearby Richmond Park. The canal was to run from Longford to Hampton Court a distance of 19 kilometers and at a cost of £4,000 – a tidy sum in those days. Amazingly this work was completed in just over nine months.

These changes were incredibly unpopular as all along its route it caused mayhem, blocking roads and dividing the lands of the parishes it crossed. Probably because of the speed in which it was constructed it was poorly finished. It leaked and was completely inadequate when heavy rain fell, leading to flooding all along its length. During the civil war its maintenance was neglected and it fell into even more disrepair. Locals took advantage of its bad state by demolishing a bridge at Longford and effectively damming the river so it dried up.

After the Restoration, King Charles II had grand plans to make Hampton Court Palace Gardens resemble a mini Versailles and had the long water built. This needed lots of water so the Longford River was resurrected. At this point another branch was also added in Bushy Park to help fill the fish ponds that Cromwell had built.

Today the Longford River is a beautiful waterway that meanders through Bushy Park, bordered by willows, sedges and rushes. It provides a fantastic wildlife habitat for perch, roach, tench and carp, as well as dragonflies and kingfishers. The carp can reach 1m in length and weigh up to 40lbs, making Bushy Park a very desirable place for fishermen, though they are are only allowed to fish on the main ponds.

It is possible to see these impressive fish in the narrow stretch of the river linking the ponds. They are particularly visible in the spring when they congregate to spawn.

Kingfishers are known to nest in Bushy Park in the quieter, undisturbed parts of the river. They like sandy banks and build a burrow up to a meter deep with a den at the end where they lay their eggs. They are a protected bird and very shy and vulnerable. The adults will not go near the nest if there is any activity nearby and so their young often starve to death. So just be satisfied with seeing an amazing flash of iridescent blue as a kingfisher whizzes by, but never go in search of a nest!!

The Longford River, near on the left, the Brick Bridge and on the right, the Iron Bridge.
Opposite page: A female kingfisher, recognised by the orange lower bill

Opposite: A tawny owl puffs up its feathers to keep warm whilst sheltering from the cold and wind in an old oak tree.

All birds struggle to find enough food in a very cold winter but kingfishers and herons find it particularly difficult if the ponds and streams are covered with ice.

The Water Gardens

The beautiful cascade and water gardens found in the north west of the park near Upper Lodge bear no resemblance to the wild mess that was there just a few years ago. This transformation is down to the dedicated work by the Friends of Bushy Park. They unearthed historical evidence of the presence of a grand baroque water feature on the site back in the 1700s and set about trying to restore the area to its former glory.

Charles Montagu, Earl of Halifax was the ranger of Bushy Park from 1709–1715. During his tenure he lived in Upper Lodge and created a very fine garden including a water feature that Charlie Dimmcock would have been proud of. Water was diverted from the Longford River to feed a cascade that flowed from an upper to a lower pond.

Two art works painted at the time were unearthed, showing the elite of the day promenading around the garden. These paintings both showed the garden in all its splendor and gave a lot of clues as to how it must have looked. The painting 'Figures in a garden' was found by Sir Roy Strong when he was doing an inventory of paintings in the Royal Collection. He stumbled upon it in a dusty storeroom in Hampton Court Palace and immediately recognised its importance. He had previously been made aware of the restoration plans for the garden and supported the work being done by The Friends. This painting, no longer confined to a dusty room, now hangs in public view in the Palace. The other painting, by Bogdani, showed in the distance, the brewhouse which provided ale to the Upper lodge estate and was also built by Charles Monagu. It has been restored as well so the vista (as depicted in the painting) is today as true to the original as possible.

By the late 1990s the ponds had been severely neglected for so long they had gone to rack and ruin. The Friends appealed for Heritage lottery funding to help with the restoration, but were turned down. However a few years later the Royal Parks tried again and this time were successful in their application.

Work began in 2008 and archaeologists were employed to uncover and record as much of the structure that remained and rebuild it as close to the original as possible. During this process 1.5 meters of silt was removed from the pond. The restored water gardens were opened to the public in October 2009, 300 years after they were originally opened, a testament to the hard work and determination of the Friends of Bushy Park.

Mistletoe

Bushy Park is blessed with a profusion of this interesting plant and is regarded as one of the best places to view it in London. Every year the Friends of Bushy and Home Park kick off their guided walk season with the 'Mistletoe Walk'.

Mistletoe is a hemi-parasitic plant meaning that it only takes fluid from it's host and does not harm or weaken the tree on which it lodges. Its seeds are encased in a sticky white substance that gets stuck to the beaks of feeding birds, particularly the blackcap. The bird then wipes its beak clean on the bark of other trees, sowing seeds unintentionally at the same time. The other bird commonly seen feeding on the berries is the mistle thrush, which gets its name from the berries on which it feasts.

Mistletoe prefers to live in lime, hawthorn and apple trees but other trees will do. The lime and hawthorn trees in Bushy Park have an abundance of mistletoe growing on them and this is a welcome addition to the parks biodiversity and provides a high quality food source for the birds that live there.

Mistletoe has a special place in the history and folklore of this and other countries throughout Europe. It has been considered as mysterious, magical and with powerful healing properties. The Druids particularly revered mistletoe growing on oak trees. At the time of the winter solstice the chief Druid would cut Mistletoe from an oak tree using a golden sickle. Sprigs would them be distributed amongst the people who put them over their doorway to protect against thunder, lightning and other evils.

Viking beliefs of Mistletoe's powers were rooted in the myth of the resurrection of Balder, the god of the summer sun. As the story goes, Balder had a dream in which he dies. The dream alarmed his mother, Frigga, the Goddess of Love and Beauty, for if Balder died, so too would all life on earth. Frigga went to all the elements, air, fire, water and earth as well as all the animals and plants on earth and asked them to spare her son. Satisfied that she had secured the cooperation of all, Frigga assured Balder that he would live forever. But Balder had one enemy, Loki, God of Evil, and Loki found one plant that Frigga had overlooked – Mistletoe. Mistletoe grows neither on the ground or under the ground – rather, it is an aerial parasite that has no roots of its own and attaches itself to the tree it grows on.

Loki made a poisoned arrow tip with the Mistletoe and tricked Balder's blind brother, Hoder, into shooting the arrow and killing Balder. For three days, the earth grew dark and the skies poured rain. Each of the elements in turn, tried to bring Balder back to life, but none were successful save for Frigga, his loving mother. Legend says that the tears she shed during those terrible three days turned into the white berries on the Mistletoe plant. In her joy at Balder's resurrection, she reversed Mistletoe's poisonous reputation, kissed everyone who passed beneath the tree on which it grew and issued a decree that should one ever pass beneath the Mistletoe, they should have a token kiss and no harm would befall them.

A mistle thrush

When Christianity took a foothold in the Celtic and Viking regions of northern Europe, the ancient ways were condemned as pagan practices and were abandoned by the newly converted. Mistletoe was one of the casualties, and for centuries it was forbidden to display the plant on Christian altars. Eventually, Mistletoe found its way back into acceptance as the Victorians revived the ancient ritual of kissing under the Mistletoe as a sign of love, romance and good luck.

Today, Mistletoe can be purchased at most flower shops and even some grocery stores at Christmas. And although we may not hold the same spiritual beliefs as the ancient Norseman and the Celts, we can always remember the good will and happiness it represents with a seasonal kiss.

Medieval farming

In medieval times, the area now covered by Bushy Park was part of the Hounslow Hundred. It was largely farmland with grazing animals and cultivated fields that were tended by the local serfs for their absent Lord of the Manor, the Mercian King, Leofric. Leofric, an insignificant character, is only remembered in history because of his infamous wife, Lady Godiva. She supposedly rode naked through the streets of Coventry in a bid to persuade her husband to reduce the exorbitant taxes that he was levying on the people. All the townspeople averted their eyes to protect her modesty, as she was doing this deed for them. Only one person spied on her: Peeping Tom – his name remains part of our language to this day. Lady Godiva, the first woman to be mentioned in the Domesday book, was a very powerful but benevolent woman. She gave much money and land to the church and it's believed that on inheriting the land in Bushy, she donated it to the newly founded Westminster Abbey.

Farming in the middle ages was pretty basic. People had only a rudimentary knowledge of how to get the best out of the land. They did practice crop rotation, however. The farmland was divided into long narrow strips and a three field system of cultivation was employed; one strip of wheat, barley or rye, one for oats, peas or beans and one was left fallow. The fields were ploughed using small oxen. The way the fields were ploughed created a series of ridges and furrows. Evidence of this type of ploughing remains today in Bushy Park, with especially good examples to be found between the Water Garden and the Woodland Gardens.

Remnants of the ridges and furrows left over from medieval farming methods still exist in the park today.

spring

Above: Not exactly the same as wildebeest crossing but an impressive site nonetheless

Left: Canal plantation

The Pheasantry and the Woodland Gardens

Every Royal park has a dog free area and in Bushy this happens to be the woodland gardens. In the year 2000 the Royal Parks, the Crown Estate, the Royal Parks Foundation and the Heritage Lottery Fund contributed £7.2 million towards the Bushy Park restoration fund. This consisted of more than 80 separate projects all with the common theme of improving the park for people, wildlife and plants. Gardens and buildings were restored, wildlife habitats were improved and better facilities and access for the public was provided. The woodland gardens were huge beneficiaries of this scheme, with money being spent on a swanky new cafe and the gardens being brought back to their former glory.

The 30 acres of fence-protected Woodland Woodland Gardens wonderfully compliment the open acid grasslands of the rest of the park and add hugely to its biodiversity. There is a large wild area in the Waterhouse Woodland gardens where dead wood has been left to rot naturally providing fabulous habitats for insects and beetles including the endangered stag beetle. The beetles eat the dead wood and lay their grubs in it and help improve soil quality.

Back in Tudor times the area was used to breed pheasants for the banquet tables of Henry VIII. Hence the cafe name of 'the pheasantry'. Originally an Asian bird, the pheasant has been a common site in England since the Norman times. There had been formal gardens on the site since the 1730s but they had been neglected. It wasn't until just after WWII when Joseph Fisher became superintendent of the park that they were resurrected. Fisher was responsible for much of the formal planting that is visible today. He liked to theme his garden and there are areas dedicated to North America and the Far East.

Ernest Wilson returned back from plant hunting in Japan at around this time and Fisher introduced many azaleas and maples from this region into his garden. He was responsible for Triss's pond, named after his daughter, and there is also a pond named after him. There are some notable trees for connoisseurs such as fine examples of the swamp cyprus from the everglades with its weird overground root system and the big cone pines also from America. Once again, after Fisher's tenure as Superintendent ended, the garden was left unattended.

The newly restored gardens are now a pleasure to wander around. Streams have been cleared of debris and the gentle cascades now flow freely. The bog garden full of giant gunera is back to it's former glory and 2000 daffodils planted by 'the Friends of Bushy Park' provide a riot of colour in the spring. Their display is followed by the cherry blossom and later the azaleas and rhododendrons. In the Autumn the maples give a show of dramatic red, orange and yellow leaves. In Fisher's day local children called the place 'fairyland' and today that name could again be used to describe this lovely space.

Heron Pond

Snowdrops and daffodils in the woodland gardens

Chestnut Avenue and Chestnut Sunday

Chestnut Avenue is a mile long avenue of horse chestnut trees, flanked on either side by four avenues of lime trees. It was the brain child of Sir Christopher Wren and runs in a straight line from Teddington to the entrance of Hampton Court Palace. It was part of the grand plans Queen Mary and King William had for the refurbishment of Hampton Court Palace.

In 1689 shortly after the pair had arrived from Holland, they visited Hampton Court and decided to give the old Tudor Palace a makeover in the style of Versailles. They employed the renowned architect Sir Christopher Wren to update the Tudor palace, but the plans were never completed because of the untimely death of Queen Mary from smallpox at the age of 33 and the subsequent death of the King in 1702. Wren's plan was to make Chestnut Avenue a grand boulevard leading to a new entrance to the palace, to the north of the Great Hall.

The avenue was finished along with the dramatic fountain as its centre piece, but the new entrance remained an architect's drawing. Wren had the title of Royal Surveyor of Works, a position that gave him lodgings near every Royal Palace. He held this position for 50 years until he was 86 and lived on and off at the house near Hampton Green for all of that time. Strictly speaking he should have given it up when he retired, but Queen Anne let him remain and he stayed there until his death. He died at the ripe old age of 90, an extraordinary age to live to in those days of rampant disease and unhygienic conditions.

In the mid 1800s Queen Victoria made Bushy Park a public park and the tradition of Chestnut Sunday began. Annually, on the Sunday nearest May 11th, when blossom on the trees should be at its peak, there is a parade and fair to celebrate the trees flowering. This was hugely popular in Victorian times and the coming of the railways to the suburbs made it possible for working class Londoners to escape the grime of the city and visit the countryside for a picnic.

This event continued every year until the start of the First World War, when it stopped for four years. It resumed after the end of the war until the Second World Way began in 1939. It may well have been the the end of Chestnut Sunday had a Hampton Wick couple, Colin and Mu Pain, not come across the tradition, while researching local history and resurrected the annual event. It is now firmly back on the annual calendar of Bushy Park and draws the crowds once again to see the beautiful trees and enjoy a day out.

The weird arial roots of the swamp cyprus trees provide support for periwinkle plants in the woodland gardens

Rabbit Stew

What have St. John's ambulance service, Bushy Park, and rabbits got in common? More than you might at first think.

In the middle of the 11C a hospice was established in Jerusalem to care for the growing numbers of Christians making the long and dangerous pilgrimage to the Holy city. This quickly developed into a hospital and over the next century a religious and military Order known as the Hospitallers of St John of Jerusalem evolved. Over the next few centuries during the various religious crusades the Order moved its headquarters from Rhodes to Malta, all the time retaining its goal of protecting and caring for pilgrims. All this good work took a great deal of funding. In 1237 Henry de St.Albans sold his Hampton land-the site of the present day Bushy Park, to the Knights. The order already owned land on the site of the palace at Hampton Court and they needed more land to increase their income to fund their humanitarian efforts.

To begin with they grazed sheep but the bottom fell out of the wool market so they looked for a more profitable use of the land and breeding rabbits was their chosen route.

Rabbits originated on the Iberian Peninsular. Phoenician merchants referred to part of Iberia as 'I-shephan-im' which means 'land of the rabbits'. This was translated as 'Hispania' or, as we know it, Spain. Romans saw the value of rabbits as a food and clothing source and started to breed them in warrens. They spread over the Roman Empire and in the year 600 Pope Gregory I in all his wisdom declared that, in fact, rabbit was not meat but fish. Therefore it was quite acceptable to eat it on fridays and during lent. This declaration led to a boom in cuniculture (rabbit raising) in France's monasteries. Rabbit is still a delicacy in France, Italy and Spain.

The legacy of all this activity is the profusion of bracken to the east of the park which grew up on the impoverished soil left behind by the grazing sheep and the plethora of rabbit burrows established by escapee rabbits who continued to live in the area. The Order of Hospitallers of St.John of Jerusalem morphed into the St. John's Ambulance Brigade, now often seen helping pilgrims on their way to worship their beloved football teams!

Left: A mandarin duck preens its feathers in the reflections of azaleas
Above: Cherry blossom in the Woodland gardens

The NPL

NPL stands for National Physical Laboratory. It is an organisation founded in 1900 and is one of the oldest standardising laboratories in the world, designed to take scientific knowledge and put it to the best use in everyday industrial and commercial life. It was due to be housed at the observatory in Kew but due to local objections this idea was abandoned and Queen Victoria donated the empty Bushy House to the Royal Society to house this new venture.

Over the years it has established itself as a world leading centre of excellence in measurement science. It has been responsible for innovations such as radar, atomic clocks and most recently the worlds first room temperature maser, whatever that may be but very important I'm sure! Many of the Britains most renowned scientists have been involved in work there, including Barnes Wallace, Alan Turing, Sir Robert Watson-Watt, Louis Essen and Donald Davies.

Barnes Wallace did early developmental work on his bouncing bomb in the research tanks at the NPL during WWII. This story was made into the film 'The Damnbusters'.

Turing was famous for his involvement in code breaking during wwII and the enigma machine which cracked the code used by German submarines. At the NPL he developed an early computer called ACE (automatic computing engine) and by some is considered the father of theoretical computer science and artificial intelligence. He was a homosexual in the days when this was still illegal and he chose to undergo hormone treatment or chemical castration as opposed to going to prison. He died from cyanide poisoning, determined as suicide, aged 42, a massive loss to the scientific community. In 2009 he was given an official public apology on behalf of the British Government for the appalling way he was treated and 4 years later the Queen granted him a posthumous pardon.

Sir Robert Watson Watt was a pioneer and significant contributor to the development of radar and as a result of successful trial experiments at the NPL a chain of radar stations was built along the south coast in time for the outbreak of war in 1939.

Louis Essen was a physicist who spent all his working life at the NPL. He worked on the precise measurement of time and determination of the speed of light and was responsible for the development of the first practical atomic clock. Accurate clocks are vital for global communications and satellite navigation.

Donald Davies developed 'packet switching' in the 1970s. This was a method of taking large amounts of data and splitting it into smaller chunks and storing it in computers. This apparently forms the basis of computer communications systems today and evolved into the internet.

Apart from all the above they also devised fail safe brakes to stop Big Ben's chiming mechanism crashing to the ground, managed to accurately weigh Concorde and helped develop graphine. Altogether a rather amazing place even if most of what they do is unintelligible to most people!

Left: an Egyptian goose

Examples of where the expression 'taking you under my wing' came from

summer

Hampton Court House

Today Hampton Court House is home to a co-educational private school during term time and is a fabulous venue for weddings and parties at weekends and during the holidays.

Situated on Hampton Court Green with its rear facade forming part of the boundary of Bushy Park, it is a beautiful house in a wonderful location. It was built in the mid-1750s by the second Earl of Halifax, George Montague-Dunk, for his mistress, Anna Marie Donaldson. He had met the singer while she was performing at London's Marylebone Gardens and was apparently so besotted with her he 'fainted with ecstasy'. He was a wealthy, influential Georgian statesman who through his dealings with North America became known as 'The Father of the Colonies'. Halifax, the capital of Nova Scotia is named after him. Mrs Donaldson's husband was offered a lucrative job in the West Indies and seemed to find no objection to his wife joining the household of the widowed George Montague as a 'governess'.

The house was designed by the renowned architect of the time, Thomas Wright. No self-respecting rich Georgian could have a house without a folly of some sort and Hampton Court House gardens came complete with a heart-shaped lake and a decorated shell grotto, the venue for many a wild party no doubt. The grotto remains, recently restored to its former glory.

The next colourful character to live in the house was John Montagu, the fourth Earl of Sandwich. It is he who is responsible for the name of the light snack we all enjoy today. Supposedly he liked a spot of gambling and would often sit at the gambling table for many hours. Instead of getting up for some food he would order his footman to bring him some beef slapped in between two slices of bread. Fellow gamblers started asking for the same thing referring to it as a 'sandwich'. Although married, he too kept a singer for a mistress: the infamous Martha Ray. She bore him at least five children and was sadly murdered by a jealous lover. Apparently, Sandwich never got over his grief. The murderer was hung for his crimes and the whole tale was immortalised in the book, 'Love and Madness' by Herbert Croft.

In the 1970s the house was the home of the Teddington Theatre Club which has now moved to the new playhouse in Hampton Hill High Street. It is sometimes used as a film location venue. In fact, Leona Lewis's video for her song 'Better in Time' was shot in the house with views over the park making an appearance towards the end.

Speedwell

Harebell

Large skipper rests on the thistle by the longford river

Top left and right: Emperor dragonflies particularly prevalent on the ponds of the Water Gardens

Bottom left: female banded demoiselle

Bottom right: Male banded demoiselle

Demoiselles are found all along the Longford River

Above: Little owl

Opposite: Red deer keeping cool and wallowing in the heat of the summer

The Deer

Bushy park is well known for its red and fallow deer herds. Red deer are the largest of the deer found in the UK and are indigenous to the country. Fallow deer are an introduced species thought to have been brought here originally by the Romans. Their numbers were increased by the Normans who stocked parks with them for hunting and they are responsible for todays large population.

In Tudor times, local parks were used for hunting deer, rabbit and hare. Bushy Park was a favourite place for Henry VIII to hunt when he was residing at Hampton Court and indeed his fellow King, William III, died of injuries he sustained in a fall whilst out hunting in Bushy Park. So the deer have been a permanent presence in the park now for many hundreds of years.

Today there are 90 red deer and 140 fallow deer in the park. They are wild, but are managed by the Park gamekeeper. To keep the herds healthy it is necessary to cull them twice a year. A male cull takes place in September and a female cull in November. Without this the herds would grow too large, leading to overgrazing and starvation.

In the winter the deer are fed with deer nuts, maize and hay to supplement what they can forage for themselves. The acorns, conkers and sweet chestnuts from trees in the park are an important part of their diet and help them build up fat reserves for the winter. The fields between the Brewhouse and the stockyard and Lime avenue are mowed to provide hay.

Most of the year the deer roam peacefully in the park. There are two exceptions to this: the rut (described later) and the other potentially more dangerous time of year (especially for dogs) is June when the young are born. They are unable to follow the herd immediately and are hidden in the bracken by their mothers who graze nearby whilst all the time keeping alert to predators. The females are very protective mothers and will think nothing of attacking a dog if it strays near. Dogs are regularly chased and have been attacked and killed, so be warned. Enjoy the deer, but respect them.

Far right: Red deer calf hide in the nettles and long grass. Don't be tempted to touch them, they haven't been abandoned, their mothers will be nearby. Red deer and fallow deer young are born with spots, the red deer subsequently lose theirs as they grow.

Leg of Mutton Pond

An evening ride for the horse rangers through the burnt out grass at the height of summer

Anyone for cricket (or cycling)?

You shouldn't be surprised when you hear about match fixing and gambling at cricket matches today. Cricket and gambling have been companions for many years. In as early as 1611 two men were prosecuted for playing cricket on Sunday, instead of going to church. By the mid 1660s it had become a major attraction for gamblers with the 'Gaming Act' of 1664 limiting the stakes of a bet to £100: a small fortune at the time. By Victorian times most villages had their own cricket team and the area around Bushy Park was no exception.

The Duke of Clarence, the future King William IV, ranger of Bushy Park and a man known to like a bit of a flutter, formed the first local cricket club, Clarence Cricket Club. There is record of a match between the MCC and Clarence Club in 1833. By the mid-1800s Bushy Park had a few cricket clubs: clubs that still remain to this day. Hampton Hill CC, Teddington CC and Hampton Wick CC all still have grounds within the park's confines and they have been joined by the more recent NPL Teddington CC. You struggle to walk around the park on a sunny Sunday without hearing the quintessential English sound of leather on willow.

Cricket isn't the only sport linked to the park. Cycling was very popular back in 1874 in Bushy Park, with the inaugural Hampton Court Great Bicycle meet. With the invention of solid rubber tyres, the old iron wheeled 'bone shaker' bikes disappeared being replaced by the 'ordinary' or 'Penny Farthing' version. By 1877, the *Scientific American* magazine reported "the largest meeting of bicycle riders that has ever been held assembled on May 25th at Hampton Court: they numbered between 1500–2000".

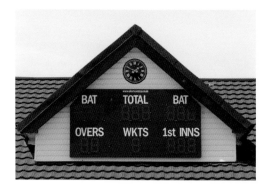

The annual meet continued to grow in popularity reaching a peak in 1882 when 2360 riders represented 183 clubs. Fast forward to 2012 and Bushy Park saw the Olympic cycling events come to town, with both the road race and the time trials race going through the park watched by thousands of excited spectators. Bradley Wiggins didn't disappoint them, winning the gold medal in the time trial. He was famously photographed after the race sitting on the winner's throne in front of Hampton Court Palace, whilst announcing he didn't actually know where he was!

The speedsters may have gone but Companion Cyclists can still be seen enjoying themselves. This lovely charity enables people with special needs to use specially adapted bicycles to pedal around the park, while taking in the beautiful scenery.

Opposite page: Sir Bradley Wiggins and Mark Cavendish during the road race at the 2012 Olympics and inset Wiggins during the time trial.

Red deer responsible for the perfect browse line of all the trees in the park

Fallow deer stag with antlers still in velvet

Struggling through the pond weed,
coots, mallards and carp

Opposite: Canal Plantation

White Lodge and the Stockyard

The Hermitage Museum and White Lodge don't appear obvious bedfellows, but there is indeed a connection. Catherine the Great of Russia had a passion for English gardens, amongst other things, and took rather a fancy to the gardening style favoured by Lancelot 'Capability' Brown, who had been appointed the post of master Gardener at Hampton Court Palace in 1764. John Spyers worked for Brown as a surveyor and did drawings and paintings of his gardens, and was a very accomplished artist. Two volumes of pictures depicting Bushy Park and Hampton Court Palace gardens were bought by Catherine and taken back to Russia, presumably to lift some of the design ideas for an English garden of her own. These volumes recently came to light having languished for years in the vast tombs of art in the basement of the Hermitage Museum in St. Petersburg. Amongst them was a water colour called a 'View of the Lodge', depicting White lodge at the end of Lime Avenue.

White lodge was built in about 1740 in a classic Georgian style and used as accommodation for a keeper of the park. Today it is a restored grade II listed building which houses the Park's administrative offices. The stockyard in which it is situated is home to the Police horses and the Companion cycling charity. There is a private area to the north between White lodge and the Upper lodge known as the brewhouse fields. This area is divided into paddocks where the horses used by the horse rangers association are turned out for a rest on a three weekly rotation. These horses are usually stabled at Hampton Court Mews just up the road. They also use the area for giving riding lessons to people with special needs in association with riding for the disabled.

Situated in front of the lodge at the end of Lime Avenue is a turf ha-ha. This is a landscape design trick that creates a recessed barrier keeping out grazing animals whist not interrupting the view. In the case of White Lodge the view is towards the Diana Statue. This technique was much employed by Capability Brown who was probably responsible for this feature that has endured.

The Diana statue is the centre piece of the park. It was commissioned by Charles I for his wife, Queen Henriett Maria. It originally stood at Somerset House but was moved to the Privy Garden at Hampton Court by Oliver Cromwell. It was moved again by Sir Christopher Wren when he redesigned Chestnut Avenue. Although called the Diana Fountain the statue actually represents Diana's nymph, Arethusa.

Lime Avenue with White Lodge at one end and the Diana fountain at the other

Hampton Hill Pond, water lilies, mallards and broad bodied chaser (dragonfly)

autumn

Lime Avenue

Any gum, Chum?

'Any gum, Chum' was apparently the cry from local children in Bushy Park during the Second World War. The long strip chewed by the Americans being preferred to the British hard-shelled lozenge. American gum was in plentiful supply on the base. This made the park a favourite destination for children when rationing hit England and sweets had become a thing of the past.

The Americans were stationed in Bushy Park in Camp Griffiss from 1942 for almost the duration of the Second World War. It was named after Lieutenant Colonel Townsend Griffiss who in 1942 was a victim of friendly fire. He was returning to England from Moscow after negotiating with Russians about a Siberian supply route for American aircraft. He was the first American airman to be shot down and killed in Europe during the war.

The camp took over large parts of the park and at one stage over 3000 American and British troops were billeted there. Dwight D. Eisenhower, a future president of America, was the Commander General of the European Theatre of Operations in charge of planning Operation Overlord, the D-Day landings. In 1943 he became Supreme Allied Commander of the Allied Expeditionary Force-SHAEF. He decided to re-locate his offices to Bushy Park, to take his men away from the distractions in Central London.

On 6th June 1944 the Normandy Landings began, the largest seabourne invasion in history with over 7,000 ships and 11,000 aircraft involved in landing 132,715 British, US and Canadian troops on the beaches of Northern France. It was considered a success despite large numbers of casualties and led to the end of the war in Europe the following summer.

On 8th May 1945 the British took over Camp Griffiss and it became headquarters of RAF transport Command and its offices were once more used to plan a major event. This time it was in 1948 and during the Cold war. Following the end of the war the allies had negotiated at Pottsdamn to split up Germany into four sections, with France, Russia, Britain and America each administering a quarter. The German Capital Berlin was also divided into four zones. In 1948 Britain, France and America united their zones into a new country: West Germany. The next day Stalin cut off all rail and road links from Berlin to West Germany – the Berlin Blockade. This led to the Berlin airlift, planned in Bushy park, where 275,000 planes transported 1.5 million tons of supplies with a plane landing every three minutes at Berlin's Templehof airport. Stalin eventually abandoned his blockade which had lasted seven months.

The camp buildings were used as a school for the children of American military personnel after the RAF left. The school shut in 1962 and the buildings were demolished much to the annoyance of local people who wanted the facilities to remain. Large demonstrations took place all to no avail and in 1963 the area was once again included in the parks boundaries. Today the area is a memorial to all the servicemen who worked within the camp with many plaques dotted around the place. There is a Heritage audio tour that can be listened to whilst exploring the site.

In preparation for the rut the velvet is shed from the antlers

Opposite: Red deer stag adorns his antlers with some brambles during the rut whilst the fallow deer stag prefers some old grass

The Rut

Most of the year the deer are calm and peaceful, tending to live in same sex groups dotted around the park. However in the Autumn all hell breaks loose. The rut, an exciting time when the deer are mating, lasts from September until November. The male red deer are in a state of testosterone fueled high tension and are much more unpredictable and aggressive than usual. They move with amazing speed and can chase a whole harem of hinds over quite a distance. Never get in between the stag and his hinds at this time and it is wise to give them all a very wide birth so their behaviour can be as natural as possible given the confines of a park. It is easy to get in their way by accident because they move about so much. A dog walk can take much longer than usual because of all the detours. Before and during the rut the stags wallow in their own urine and their odour helps bring the hinds into oestrus. 'Eau de stag' is potent stuff.

The red deer males will posture by bellowing and grunting and walking in parallel with rivals in a show of strength. If neither stag backs down a fight can ensue in which severe injuries can be received. Once a stag has proved his dominance he will guard his harem of hinds so no other male can mate with them.

During this time they hardly eat and can lose up to 20% of their body weight. The fallow deer employ a slightly different technique depending on the habitat and density of the deer population. They sometimes make a rutting stand and wait for the does to come to them to form a harem or alternatively a few bucks will have just a few does with them as in a 'lek'. The fighting process is similar to the red deer.

Antlers are extensions of the skull of the deer. In April the males of both Red and Fallow species lose their antlers and immediately start to grow a new set and they are the only mammalian organs that can fully regenerate each year. The boney appendage is covered in a fine furry material called velvet which is full of blood vessels providing nourishment and oxygen to the growing antlers.

Antler bone is one of the fastest known types of tissue growth in mammals, growing at a rate of up to 10mm a day. When the antlers have stopped growing the velvet falls off and the soft bone hardens ready for action in the rut.

The larger the antlers the more likelihood of sexual selection. Problems with the antlers usually indicate some problem with the testicles and reproductive prowess of the stag. Each year the new set of antlers are bigger and better than last years.

The red deer have spikes or tines on their antlers, which denote the approximate age of the animal. This is only a rough estimate though because the wild stags in Scotland have a much harsher life foraging than our pampered park deer and their antlers are much smaller in comparison. The fallow deer are the only type of deer in the UK with palmate or flat antlers. These develop when the male is in excess of three years old.

Upper Lodge and the Water Gardens

Chestnuts provide food for the deer in the Autumn

Upper Lodge

Upper Lodge, situated near the Hampton Hill gate entrance to the park, is the oldest occupied site in the park. It almost certainly started life as a small Roman marching fort, commanding the bend in the river from Teddington to Hampton.

During the following years the Anglo Saxons probably used the site as their manor house as the area surrounding the present day house still has clear evidence of ridge and furrow ploughing systems so beloved by the farmers of that era.

The first records of a dwelling on the site are from 1537. Various keepers of the park lived there intermittently for the next couple of hundred years. But it wasn't until 1709 when Charles Montagu, 1st Earl of Halifax purchased the keepership of the parks at Hampton Court that the house became significant.

He inherited a house in the state of dilapidation that needed demolishing and re-building. He set about this with gusto but his most important contribution to the park was his beautiful Water Garden, grandly situated in front of the house.

He also built the brewhouse and planted orchards. Charles Montagu's other claim to fame is that he was responsible for creating a joint stock company that became the bank of England in 1694, which marked the beginning of funded national debt. The lodge stayed in the Halifax family until William, Duke of Clarence, succeeded as Ranger.

After the First World War, King George V gave permission for Upper Lodge to become a convalescent home for Canadian troops. Later he granted the building to the London County Council as a holiday school for East End boys with respiratory diseases. 280 poor boys were housed in the former hospital dormitories, given lessons out of doors and encouraged to swim in the pools of the Water Gardens.

In 1944 General Eisenhower requisitioned part of the camp as the Supreme Headquarters of the Allied Expeditionary Force (SHAEF).

Upper Lodge was transferred in 1945 from the Air Ministry to the Admiralty, who dug the Admiralty Cut to divert the Longford River from feeding the pools at Upper Lodge. The still water in the upper pool was then used for testing mines. The Ministry of Defence finally relinquished the lease to The Crown Estate in 1994.

The cascade and Water Gardens have subsequently been restored to their former glory and are now one of the main attractions in the park.

Honey fungus in the Water Gardens

Dew-laden spiders' webs

Hampton Hill Pond

Bushy House

The site of the present Bushy House probably started life as a stand for the gambling public of the time to watch rabbit coursing, the forerunner to greyhound racing, which was immensely popular at the time.

In 1663 Edward Proger was ordered by King Charles II to 'build a lodge for our service in one of our parks at Hampton Court'. No expense was spared and the design was a fine example of the architecture that became fashionable after the restoration. Proger was a loyal servant and friend to the king and went into exile in France with him when he fled England after defeat by Cromwell. He acted as go-between in the king's relationships with his many mistresses and it has been suggested that Bushy house was built as a rendevous for the King and his lovers. It was considered far too grand to be just a keepers lodge. One of the disgarded mistresses became Progers wife and after Charles died Proger retired to Bushy house and lived there until he died at the ripe old age of 92. He held the post of keeper of the park for 48 years.

Over the years prominent members of the aristocracy lived in the house holding the position of Keeper of the park. Lord North, Chancellor of the exchequer and leader of the House of Commons during the reign of George III, moved his family there after resigning from government because of his abject handling of the American War of Independence, and his wife held the office of Keeper.

The next Ranger was William, Duke of Clarence, third son of George III. A colourful character, who had spent his formative years at sea was not seen as a future king. He was given Bushy Park to oversee and possibly keep him out of mischief. He moved in with his mistress the comedy actress Dora Jordan and their three illegitimate children.Over the next 20 years a further seven children were born while they lived together at Bushy House. The Duke, always short of money, had the Tudor oaks, amongst other trees, felled – a total of 758 trees altogether – and sold for a good profit, changing the profile of the park completely.

The Duke joined in with local life, spending time drinking and playing cards at nearby inns, watching cricket and boxing matches, which endeared him to the Hampton residents. Dora's earnings helped keep them in a style to which they were accustomed but as she aged her earning power diminished.

This coincided with ill health of the heirs to the throne making it a possibility that William may indeed become King. Unfortunately Dora had to go. She was packed off with an allowance with the proviso that she should not perform any more. Once the powers that be found out that she had reneged on this deal, they cut off her money and she died a pauper in France. Her children by the king took on the name FitzClarence and our present prime minister David Cameron is one of her descendants.

William found a rich wife, Princess Adelaide of Saxe-Meiningen who helped him out with his financial problems and provided him with a legitimate heir. They seemed to be very happy but the poor woman had many miscarriages and children who died at a young age, so when William IV died his niece Victoria took over as Queen. Adelaide remained at Bushy Park giving generously to local good causes, including gifts of beef and bread at christmas to 800 local poor families. She was held in great affection and her death in 1849 was much mourned. After her death it became apparent that she had donated nearly half her income to local charities.

Next resident of the house was the exiled Duc de Nemours, son of the exiled King of France fleeing the revolution. After his death it was returned to the crown. Queen Victoria had no use for it and it was given to the National Physical Laboratory in whose hands it remains today.

Autumn colour in the Woodland Gardens

Mist over the Brewhouse fields

index

First Edition – © Unity Print and Publishing Limited 2014

Designed by Ball Design Consultancy, www.balldesignconsultancy.com

Printed by Page Brothers of Norwich, Norfolk. www.pagebros.co.uk

Colour Management by Paul Sherfield of The Missing Horse Consultancy. www.missinghorsecons.co.uk

Publishing Assistant: Jessica Dean

Published by Andrew Wilson, Unity Print and Publishing Limited, 18 Dungarvan Avenue, London SW15 5QU.
Tel: +44 (0)20 8487 2199 aw@unity-publishing.co.uk www.unity-publishing.co.uk Twitter: @andrewpics

Bushy Park

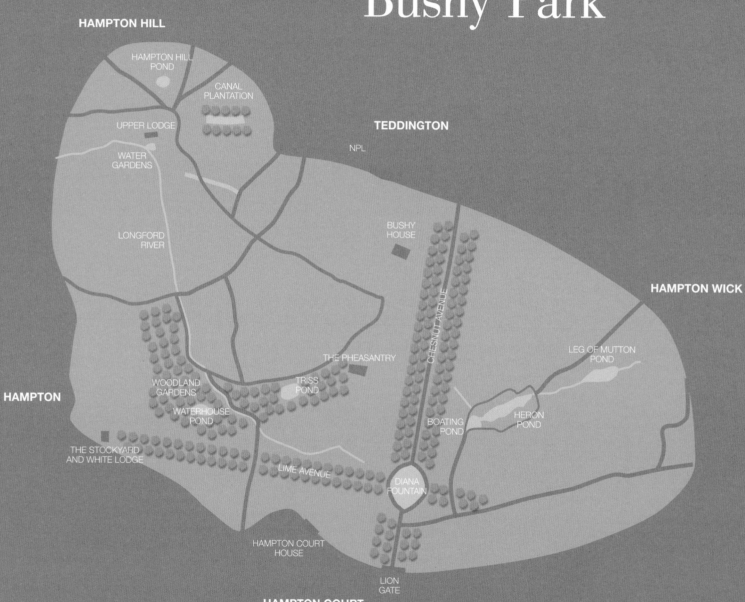